A **Literature Kit**™ FOR

The Grapes of Wrath

By John Steinbeck

Written by Gideon Jagged

GRADES 9 - 12

Classroom Complete Press
P.O. Box 19729
San Diego, CA 92159
Tel: 1-800-663-3609 | Fax: 1-800-663-3608
Email: service@classroomcompletepress.com

www.classroomcompletepress.com

ISBN – 13: 978-1-55319-974-8

 We acknowledge the financial support of the Government of Canada through the Canadian Book Fund for our publishing activities.

Critical Thinking Skills

The Grapes of Wrath

Level	Skills for Critical Thinking	1–5	6–9	10–13	14–16	17–19	20–21	22–23	24–25	26–27	28–30	Writing Tasks	Graphic Organizers
		Chapter Questions											
LEVEL 1 Remembering	• Identify Story Elements	✓	✓	✓	✓	✓	✓	✓	✓	✓	✓	✓	✓
	• Recall Details	✓	✓	✓	✓	✓	✓	✓	✓	✓	✓	✓	✓
	• Match	✓	✓	✓	✓		✓	✓			✓		✓
	• Sequence Events		✓				✓				✓		✓
LEVEL 2 Understanding	• Compare & Contrast	✓				✓		✓	✓	✓		✓	✓
	• Summarize	✓	✓	✓	✓	✓	✓	✓	✓	✓	✓		✓
	• State Main Idea				✓	✓	✓	✓				✓	✓
	• Describe	✓	✓	✓	✓	✓	✓	✓	✓	✓	✓	✓	✓
	• Classify	✓				✓	✓		✓		✓		✓
LEVEL 3 Applying	• Plan			✓	✓	✓	✓	✓	✓	✓	✓	✓	✓
	• Interview											✓	
	• Infer Outcomes	✓	✓	✓	✓	✓	✓			✓		✓	✓
LEVEL 4 Analysing	• Draw Conclusions	✓	✓	✓	✓	✓	✓	✓	✓	✓	✓	✓	✓
	• Identify Supporting Evidence	✓	✓	✓	✓	✓	✓	✓	✓	✓	✓	✓	✓
	• Motivations	✓	✓	✓	✓	✓	✓	✓	✓	✓	✓	✓	✓
	• Identify Cause & Effect						✓	✓				✓	✓
LEVEL 5 Evaluating	• State & Defend an Opinion	✓	✓	✓	✓	✓	✓	✓	✓	✓	✓	✓	✓
	• Make Judgements	✓	✓	✓	✓	✓		✓	✓	✓	✓	✓	✓
LEVEL 6 Creating	• Predict	✓	✓	✓	✓	✓		✓		✓	✓	✓	
	• Design			✓	✓	✓		✓	✓	✓	✓	✓	
	• Create			✓	✓			✓	✓	✓	✓	✓	✓
	• Imagine Alternatives		✓	✓	✓	✓	✓	✓		✓	✓	✓	

Based on Bloom's Taxonomy

Contents

TEACHER GUIDE

STUDENT HANDOUTS

Assessment Rubric

The Grapes of Wrath

Student's Name: ____________ Assignment: ____________ Level: ____________

	Level 1	Level 2	Level 3	Level 4
Comprehension of Novel	Demonstrates a limited understanding of the novel	Demonstrates some understanding of the novel	Demonstrates a considerable understanding of the novel	Demonstrates a thorough understanding of the novel
Content • Information and details relevant to focus	Elements incomplete; key details missing	Some elements are complete; details missing	All required elements complete; key details contain some description	All required elements are complete; enough description for clarity
Style • Effective word choice and originality • Precise language	Little variety in word choice. Language vague and imprecise	Some variety in word choice. Language somewhat vague and imprecise	Good variety in word choice. Language precise and quite descriptive	Writer's voice is apparent throughout. Excellent choice of words. Precise language
Conventions • Spelling, language, capitalization, punctuation	Errors seriously interfere with the writer's purpose	Repeated errors in mechanics and usage	Some errors in convention	Few errors in convention

STRENGTHS:

WEAKNESSES:

NEXT STEPS:

Teacher Guide

*Our resource has been created for ease of use by both **TEACHERS** and **STUDENTS** alike.*

Introduction

Our literature kit is designed to give the teacher a number of helpful ways of making the study of this novel a more enjoyable and profitable experience for the students. Our guide features a number of useful and flexible components, from which the teacher can choose. It is not expected that all of the activities will be completed.

One advantage to this approach to the study of a novel is that the student can work at his or her own speed, and the teacher can assign activities that match the student's abilities.

Our literature kit divides the novel by chapters and features reading comprehension and vocabulary questions. Themes include survival, strength in unity, and rebirth. The Grapes of Wrath *provides a wealth of opportunity for classroom discussion because it presents the conflict between those with money and those without in a vivid, visceral way. Moral and social justice and the role of law in maintaining a system seen as unjust is certain to evoke passionate and conflicting views.*

How Is Our Literature Kit™ Organized?

STUDENT HANDOUTS

Chapter Activities *(in the form of reproducible worksheets)* make up the majority of this resource. For each group of chapters, there are BEFORE YOU READ activities and AFTER YOU READ activities.

- The BEFORE YOU READ activities prepare students for reading by setting a purpose for reading. They stimulate background knowledge and experience, and guide students to make connections between what they know and what they will learn. Important concepts and vocabulary from the chapter(s) are also presented.
- The AFTER YOU READ activities check students' comprehension and extend their learning. Students are asked to give thoughtful consideration of the text through creative and evaluative short-answer questions and journal prompts.

Six **Writing Tasks** and three **Graphic Organizers** are included to further develop students' critical thinking and writing skills, and analysis of the text. *(See page 6 for suggestions on using the Graphic Organizers.)* The **Assessment Rubric** *(page 4)* is a useful tool for evaluating students' responses to the Writing Tasks and Graphic Organizers.

PICTURE CUES

This resource contains three main types of pages, each with a different purpose and use. A **Picture Cue** at the top of each page shows, at a glance, what the page is for.

Teacher Guide
- Information and tools for the teacher

Student Handout
- Reproducible worksheets and activities

Easy Marking™ Answer Key
- Answers for student activities

EASY MARKING™ ANSWER KEY

Marking students' worksheets is fast and easy with this **Answer Key**. Answers are listed in columns—just line up the column with its corresponding worksheet, as shown, and see how every question matches up with its answer!

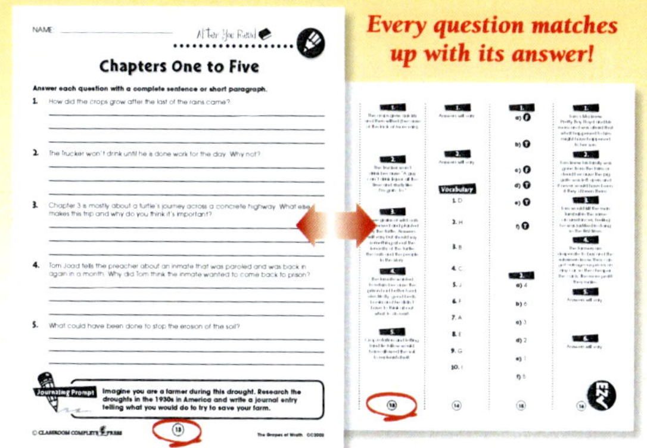

1, 2, 3
Graphic Organizers

The three **Graphic Organizers** included in this **Literature Kit™** are especially suited to a study of ***The Grapes of Wrath***. Below are suggestions for using each organizer in your classroom, or they may also be adapted to suit the individual needs of your students. The organizers can be used on a projection system or interactive whiteboard in teacher-led activities, and/or photocopied for use as student worksheets. To evaluate students' responses to any of the organizers, you may wish to use the **Assessment Rubric** *(on page 4)*.

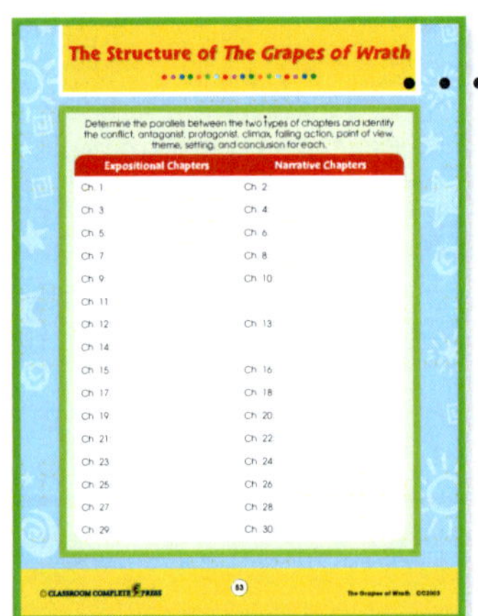

THE STRUCTURE OF *THE GRAPES OF WRATH*

This activity should follow a discussion of the narrative structure of the novel. The narrative chapters themselves form a coherent story on their own. The intercalary chapters are largely expositional and place the struggle in the larger context of the Depression Era and the Dust Bowl. This activity should be a discussion centered on the parallels between the two types of chapters and how the structure applies to the latter type; what Chapters 19 and 20 have in common and the identity of the protagonist of the intercalary chapters, for example. **Found on Page 53.**

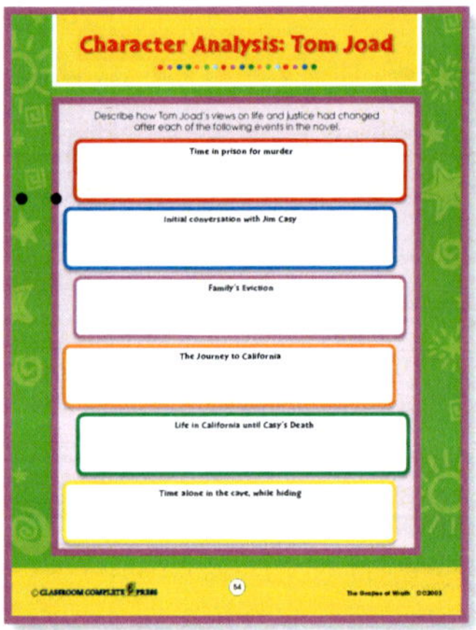

CHARACTER ANALYSIS: TOM JOAD

Tom Joad, the protagonist of the novel, undergoes a profound change as the events that change his life and the lives of his family unfold. This activity should be a discussion of those changes, as they happen. **Found on Page 54.**

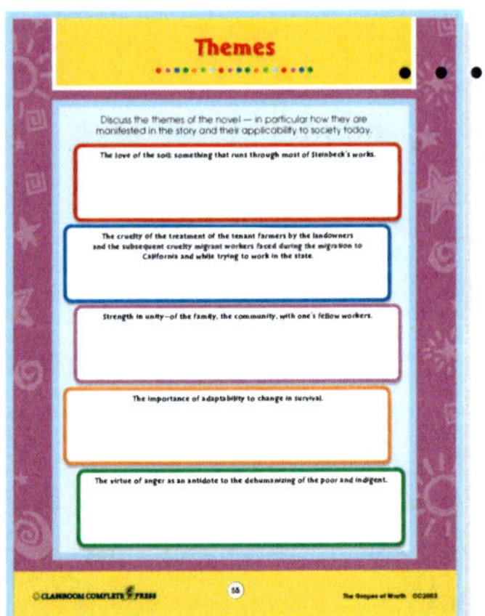

THEMES

After the novel has been read, a discussion of the themes should be had. The major themes are:

- The love of the soil.
- The cruelty of the treatment of the tenant farmers by the landowners and the subsequent cruelty migrant workers faced during the migration to California and while trying to work in the state.
- Strength in unity — of the family, the community, with one's fellow workers.
- The importance of adaptability to change in the equation of survival.
- The virtue of anger as an antidote to the dehumanizing of the poor and needy. **Found on Page 55.**

Bloom's Taxonomy* for Reading Comprehension

The activities in this resource engage and build the full range of thinking skills that are essential for students' reading comprehension. Based on the six levels of thinking in Bloom's Taxonomy, questions are given that challenge students to not only recall what they have read, but to move beyond this to understand the text through higher-order thinking. By using higher-order skills of applying, analyzing, evaluating and creating, students become active readers, drawing more meaning from the text, and applying and extending their learning in more sophisticated ways.

This **Literature Kit™**, therefore, is an effective tool for any Language Arts program. Whether it is used in whole or in part, or adapted to meet individual student needs, this resource provides teachers with the important questions to ask, inspiring students' interest and creativity, and promoting meaningful learning.

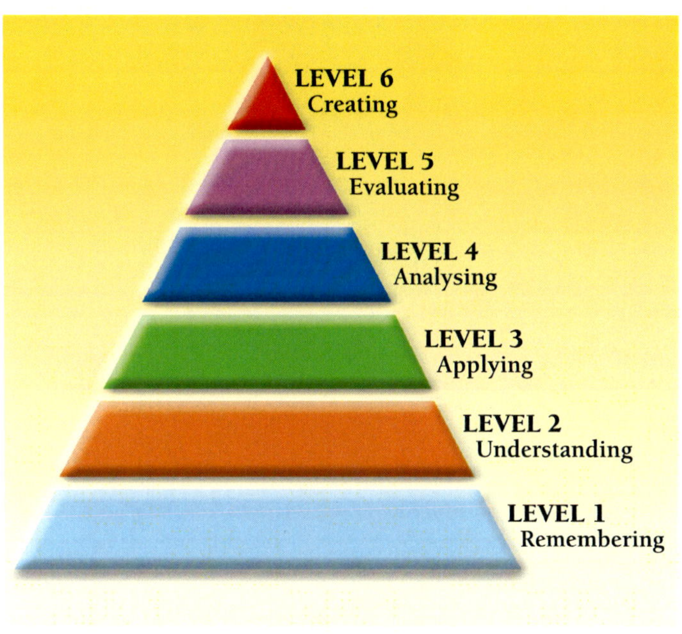

BLOOM'S TAXONOMY: 6 LEVELS OF THINKING

**Bloom's Taxonomy is a widely used tool by educators for classifying learning objectives, and is based on the work of Benjamin Bloom.*

Teaching Strategies

WHOLE-CLASS, SMALL GROUP AND INDEPENDENT STUDY

This study guide contains the following activities:

Before Reading Activities: themes are introduced and thought-provoking questions put forward for the students to consider.

Vocabulary Activities: new and unfamiliar words are introduced and reviewed.

After Reading Questions: the first part of this section includes short answer questions dealing with the content of the text. The second part features questions that are more open-ended and feature concepts from the higher order of Bloom's Taxonomy.

Writing Tasks: creative writing assignments based on Bloom's Taxonomy that relate to the plot of the particular chapters.

A comprehension quiz is also included comprised of multiple-choice, true/false and short-answer questions.

Graphic Organizers: three full-page reproducible sheets have been included and can be used for teaching purposes throughout the text.

Bonus Sheets are also available online.

The study guide can be used in a variety of ways in the classroom depending on the needs of the students and teacher. The teacher may choose to use an independent reading approach with students capable of working independently. It also works well with small groups, with most of the lessons being quite easy to follow. Finally, in other situations, teachers will choose to use it with their entire class.

Teachers may wish to have their students keep a daily reading log so that they might record their daily progress and reflections.

Summary of the Story

The Grapes of Wrath *by John Steinbeck is the story of one family's migration from their Oklahoma farm to California during the Great Depression in search of a better life. The Joad family is just one of thousands who work the land they do not own. They are forced off by the owners of the land because drought and over-farming have made it largely infertile. They decide to make their way to the west coast, where they have been told good jobs and high wages await them.*

After a difficult journey, which sees the death of the older family members and the loss of most of their money, the Joads realize they have been lied to. A quarter million other refugees from the Dust Bowl (as the disaster has been labeled) also want work. The landowners are paying less than a living wage and there are much fewer jobs than there are people trying to get them.

The novel ends with no clear resolution. The Joad family is largely scattered by the end, but it does conclude with a strong message about the need for compassion and unity, especially in the face of starvation.

Suggestions for Further Reading

OTHER BOOKS BY JOHN STEINBECK

In Dubious Battle © 1936
Of Mice and Men © 1937
Cannery Row © 1945
East of Eden © 1952
The Winter of Our Discontent © 1961
Travels with Charley: In Search of America © 1962

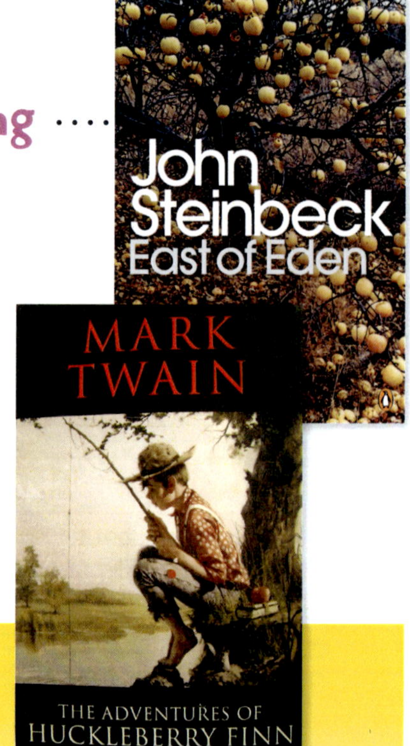

OTHER RECOMMENDED RESOURCES

Mark Twain, ***Adventures of Huckleberry Finn*** © 1884
Stephen Crane, ***The Red Badge of Courage*** © 1895
Ernest Hemingway, ***The Sun Also Rises*** © 1926
Pearl S. Buck, ***The Good Earth*** © 1931
Carey McWilliams, ***Factories In The Field: The Story of Migratory Farm Labor in California*** © 1939
James N. Gregory, ***American Exodus: The Dust Bowl Migration and Okie Culture in California*** © 1989
Timothy Egan, ***The Worst Hard Time*** © 2006

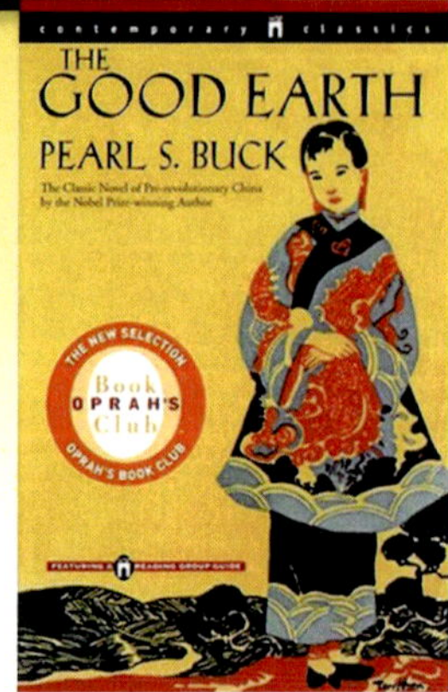

List of Vocabulary

CHAPTERS 1 TO 5

• recrossed • rainheads • rootlets • emulsion • hasp • chambray • cropper • proboscis • foxtails • anlage • embankment • parapet • scrawny • declivity • speckled • fallow • tenant • subnosed • germinate • sheathing

CHAPTERS 6 TO 9

• trough • truculent • cottontails • tractored • senselessness • drone • skittering • sheaf • jalopies • intensifier • glinting • daintily • blazes • cantankerous • misshapen • oilcloth • surveyed • veneration • rakish • premium

CHAPTERS 10 TO 13

• puckered • provocatively • whirling • singletrees • talcum • panoramically • phosphates • vacant • tributary • heifer • chattering • swarmed • whisked • watery • wizened • mattock • transgression • gulch • scampered

CHAPTERS 14 TO 16

• multiplied • bewildered • spatula • turntable • waxpapered • streamlined • buzzard • lax • flush • babbitt • corrugated • piston • gasket • proprietor • dungarees • contractor • coroner • clod

CHAPTERS 17 TO 19

• timid • courtesies • drowsed • encampment • snorting • puckering • exhortation • muskrat • decorous • tarpaulin • illuminated • scuttled • comforter • frantic • accumulation • gunny • jabbering • dispossessed • cemented

CHAPTERS 20 TO 21

• slovenly • snooped • vagrant • hereabouts • comporting • mechanically • squinted • circuitousness • resentment • glistened • unkempt • clanked • flywheel • degenerate • mold • debtless • cannery • handbills • granaries

CHAPTERS 22 TO 23

• watchman • quarrelsome • shirtwaist • sugared • wriggling • agitators • spittily • fistfuls • cornmeal • gingham • stringy • mammoth • unanimous • reverential • raddled • triumphantly • headband • sycamores • haycock

CHAPTERS 24 TO 25

• friction • Panhandle • engagingly • bristled • vibrant • fruitfulness • cultivators • tannic • denunciation • symbolize • pellagra • irrigation • formic • putrescence • rattling • putrefying • ooze • yellowjackets • mash

CHAPTERS 26 TO 27

• splinter • temples • adjoining • squirmed • spluttered • sullenness • roadster • side-meat • splattering • forlornly • khaki • windfalls • belligerently • contemptuously • wolfishly • stubble • prostrate • smothered • angling • inquisitive

CHAPTERS 28 TO 30

• stout • pitched • cricking • boxcar • paling • screeched • spurted • grapevine • lusterless • brokenly • cottonwoods • mastoids • utensils • floundered • metallic • scooped • elaborate • cultivator • mysteriously

John Steinbeck

John Steinbeck (1902–1968), was born to a family of modest means in Salinas, California. He attended Stanford University, though he never received a degree. Beginning in 1925, John tried to earn a living as a freelance writer in New York. After failing to do so, he returned to California where he wrote and published his first novels and short stories. It was a collection of comedic short stories about Monterey paisanos, *Tortilla Flat* (1935) that first gained him some degree of recognition.

For the most part, Steinbeck wrote social novels that dealt with rural labor and the economic problems that go along with it. It has been noted that his works also express a reverence for the soil and the people who work it that is sometimes at odds with the sociological bent of his books as a whole. After the coarse humor of his first hit novel, Steinbeck wrote something a good deal more serious. *In Dubious Battle* (1936) was an aggressively critical social novel dealing with migratory fruit pickers on California plantations and their strikes for better conditions and wages. After this, he wrote *Of Mice and Men* (1937), which told the tale of Lennie, a very large man who was an imbecile. Next was *The Long Valley* (1938), a series of excellent short stories. *The Grapes of Wrath*, published in 1939, is widely considered to be his best work. It is the story of tenant farmers in Oklahoma who, after being forced from their land that is becoming infertile, migrate along with hundreds of thousands of others to California to get work.

Steinbeck wrote several good novels in his later years, the most outstanding of which are *East of Eden* (1952), *The Winter of Our Discontent* (1961), and *Travels with Charley* (1962). The latter is an account of Steinbeck's travels in a truck through forty U.S. states over a three month period. He died in 1968 in New York City.

Did You Know?

- **Steinbeck was the most popular deceased American writer in the mid-1990s; his works sold 750,000 annually.**
- **American literary critics thought he was undeserving of the Nobel Prize for Literature that he won in 1962.**
- **For most of his life, Steinbeck would draw a pig with wings after his signature. He named it Pigasus. Pigasus symbolized Steinbeck as "earthbound but aspiring.... A lumbering soul but trying to fly... (with)... not enough wingspread but plenty of intention."**

NAME: ______________________________

Chapters One to Five

Answer the questions in complete sentences.

1. This story is about the devastating effects of drought on those who make their livelihood from farming. What else can adversely affect crop growth?

____

____

____

2. Besides farming, what other industries do you think would be affected by drought?

____

____

____

Vocabulary

Choose a word from the list that means the same or nearly the same as the underlined word. Be careful—a couple are a bit tricky!

emulsion	**chambray**	**proboscis**	**parapet**
fallow	**germinate**	**sheathing**	**declivity**

☐ **1.** When she first saw it, Tiffany thought the elephant's **trunk** was a snake.

☐ **2.** The porcelain teapot was covered in a **jacket** of blue wool.

☐ **3.** Getting the golf ball into the hole was going to be tough as it was currently at the bottom of an **incline**.

☐ **4.** Jim wore a **denim** shirt to his first day of work.

☐ **5.** It took the twenty men, eighteen hours to erect a **bulwark** of sandbags to protect the neighborhood against the flooding river.

☐ **6.** George's father decided to leave the back ten acres of his farm **untilled** this season.

☐ **7.** It took most of the semester for the ideas Jill learned in math class to begin to **develop** into a real understanding of trigonometry.

☐ **8.** If too little sand is in the water, it will not be in **suspension** and you don't have good mud pies.

NAME: ____________________

Chapters One to Five

1. Put a check mark (✓) next to the answer that is most correct.

a) How long did the wind blow?

- ◯ **A** 1.5 days
- ◯ **B** 2 days
- ◯ **C** 1 day
- ◯ **D** 2.5 days

b) The trucker describes another trucker doing what while driving?

- ◯ **A** Singing
- ◯ **B** Writing stories
- ◯ **C** Writing poetry
- ◯ **D** Sketching

c) When the woman driving the sedan drove by, she:

- ◯ **A** didn't see the turtle until it was too late.
- ◯ **B** swerved to hit the turtle.
- ◯ **C** saw the turtle but didn't do anything.
- ◯ **D** swerved to avoid the turtle.

d) Why did Casy stop being a preacher?

- ◯ **A** He decided there was no God.
- ◯ **B** He realized it was people he believed in.
- ◯ **C** He thought he was too sinful to be a preacher.
- ◯ **D** He didn't want people hurting themselves because of him.

e) When the men told the farmers they had to get off the land, who did they blame?

- ◯ **A** The banks
- ◯ **B** The weather
- ◯ **C** God
- ◯ **D** The owners

NAME: ______________________

Chapters One to Five

Answer each question with a complete sentence or short paragraph.

1. How did the crops grow after the last of the rains came?

2. The trucker won't drink until he is done work for the day. Why not?

3. Chapter 3 is mostly about a turtle's journey across a concrete highway. What else makes this trip and why do you think it's important?

4. Tom Joad tells the preacher about an inmate that was paroled and was back in again in a month. Why did Tom think the inmate wanted to come back to prison?

5. What could have been done to stop the erosion of the soil?

Imagine you are a farmer during this drought. Research the droughts in the 1930s in America and write a journal entry telling what you would do to try to save your farm.

NAME: ______________________

Chapters Six to Nine

Answer the questions in complete sentences.

1. If you were one of the farmers who had been told that they had to vacate their land immediately, what would you have done? Why?

____

____

2. If you ran a business selling things that the farmers needed, you would be in trouble. Do you think you would try to help the farmers by lowering prices and or extending credit? Why or why not?

____

____

Vocabulary

With a straight line, connect each word on the left with its meaning on the right.

1	**truculent**	Badly formed; deformed	A
2	**skittering**	A bundle of cut stalks of grain or similar plants bound with straw or twine	B
3	**sheaf**	Something that increases, sharpens, or makes something denser or stronger	C
4	**intensifier**	Feeling or displaying ferocity: cruel, savage	D
5	**glinting**	Inspected carefully; scrutinized	E
6	**cantankerous**	Difficult or irritating to deal with	F
7	**misshapen**	Respect or awe for a person or thing	G
8	**surveyed**	Moving rapidly along a surface with frequent light contacts or changes of direction	H
9	**veneration**	A prize, bonus or award given as an inducement	I
10	**premium**	Momentarily flashing or sparkling	J

NAME: ______________________________

Chapters Six to Nine

1. Circle **T** if the statement is TRUE or **F** if it is FALSE.

T F a) After their farm was taken from them, the Joads had no way to make money to go west.

T F b) Tom's father is worried about his brother Al because all he cares about are cars and girls.

T F c) The Joads got decent prices for their farming equipment.

T F d) No one was selling decent cars cheaply.

T F e) Muley didn't go with his family because he couldn't bear to abandon his land.

T F f) Tom's Ma was worried that Tom might have become crazy mad in prison.

2. Number the events from **1** to **6** in the order they occurred in these chapters.

☐ **a)** Tom and Casy reach Uncle John's farm.

☐ **b)** Casy says grace before the Joad family meal.

☐ **c)** Muley Graves tells Tom his family is at his Uncle John's.

☐ **d)** Tom, Casy and Muley spend the night in a cave.

☐ **e)** Tom finds his family's home wrecked and abandoned.

☐ **f)** Tom surprises his mother by walking into the kitchen unannounced.

After You Read

NAME: ______________________________

Chapters Six to Nine

Answer each question with a complete sentence.

1. What made Tom's mother worried that Tom might be crazy mad because of his time in prison?

____

____

2. What led Tom to believe that his parents were either gone from the family farm or dead?

____

____

3. Tom was jailed for killing a man in a fight. Would he do it again after his time in prison? Why or why not?

____

____

4. Why aren't the car salesmen interested in selling anything other than old wrecks to the farmers who are leaving?

____

____

5. Casy and Tom tell Muley that they don't think he's "touched" (crazy), yet they both think he is. Why do you think they lied to him?

____

____

6. Anything of sentimental value that could not be taken or sold was burned. Why do you think that is?

____

____

Imagine that you are told you have to leave your home and can only take with you whatever will fit into a carry-on bag. Write a journal entry starting after you're on your way, telling what you took and what you had to leave behind, focusing on how hard some choices were.

NAME: ______________________________

Chapters Ten to Thirteen

Answer the questions in complete sentences.

1. No one thinks of going anywhere other than to California, despite their misgivings. Why do you think that is?

____

____

____

2. Many families are moving west in this story. Do you think that will make things harder for the Joads? Why or why not?

____

____

____

Vocabulary

Complete each sentence with a word from the list.

provocatively	**talcum**	**vacant**	**tributary**
whisked	**wizened**	**mattock**	**gulch**

1. The doctor told Jeremy that ____________ would help stop the rash.

2. There was no need to bring a pick and a shovel when the toolshed had a perfectly good ____________ in it.

3. Sarah's minister had warned her repeatedly of the dangers of dressing so ____________.

4. The ____________ lot beside the hardware store was a perfect place to play kickball.

5. Most of the apples in the barrel were either rotten or ____________.

6. The water from the burst main had cut a winding ____________ through the sandy soil of the park next door.

7. John ____________ everything off the table with a sweep of his arm.

8. As large as the river was, it was only a ____________ of the even larger one it merged with a few miles down.

NAME: ______________________________

Chapters Ten to Thirteen

1. Fill in each blank with the correct word from the chapters.

a) And the world was ___________ to her; she thought only in terms of reproduction and of motherhood.

b) The kitchen became a ___________ of heat, and the family ate hurriedly, and went out to sit on the doorstep until the water should get hot.

c) The man who is more than his chemistry, walking on the earth, turning his plow point for a stone, dropping his handles to slide over an ___________, kneeling in the earth to eat his lunch; that man who is more than his elements knows the land that is more than its analysis.

d) They built a trailer out of ___________ and loaded it with their possessions.

e) And inside the open door of the shack Tom saw the oil barrels, only two of them, and the candy counter with stale candies and ___________ whips turning brown with age, and cigarettes.

2. Complete each sentence with a word from the list.

puckered	heifer	chattering	transgression	scampered

a) To Dave, the squawking of the turkeys sounded like the ____________ of his sisters at Sunday dinner.

b) The skin around the wound in Sheila's arm was ____________.

c) The younger children didn't wait to be told that class was over before they ____________ out the door to play.

d) Albert asked if he was going to be fired and was told his ____________ wasn't as serious as all that.

e) There were three young cows in the field, but Dennis was told the only ____________ was the one in the middle.

NAME: ______________________

Chapters Ten to Thirteen

Answer each question with a complete sentence.

1. What did the family do to save money on food for the first part of their journey?

2. Why did Muley really stop by just before the Joads left for California?

3. Who came to visit the houses of the farmers after they left?

4. What part of the trip was Al most worried about? Why?

5. Why wasn't Tom worried about breaking his parole by crossing state lines?

6. According to Casy, why did Grampa Joad die?

If you were left behind after everyone in your neighborhood left, what would you do to survive? Write a journal entry telling about your first day on your own.

NAME: ______________________________

Chapters Fourteen to Sixteen

Answer the questions in complete sentences.

1. With several hundred thousand people streaming into California looking for work, how do you think the people living there, especially the landowners, will react?

____
____
____

2. What do you think the Joads will do if they can't find work in California? What *should* they do?

____
____
____

Vocabulary

Complete each sentence with a word from the list.

bewildered	**streamlined**	**corrugated**	**gasket**
proprietor	**dungarees**	**contractor**	**coroner**

1. Mike's mom scolded him for wearing his good pants on the playground, telling him he should have worn his old ____________ instead.
2. The drainage culverts were made of concrete rather than the ____________ iron he had expected.
3. The doctor assured the family that the death was from natural causes and therefore a ____________ would not be required.
4. The homeowners did much of the work themselves but had a ____________ build the deck.
5. Jim's car probably would get much better gas mileage if it were better ____________.
6. The purple top hat her mom was wearing while she cooked dinner had Janine completely ____________.
7. The puddle of soup in the vegetable crisper indicated to David that the ____________ on the Mason jar was missing—again.
8. Jim's complaints got him no satisfaction for, as the mechanic explained, the garage's ____________ was out of town on vacation.

NAME: ______________________________

Chapters Fourteen to Sixteen

Fill in each blank with the correct word from the chapters.

a) This you may say of man—when theories change and crash, when schools, __________, when narrow dark alleys of thought, national, religious, economic, grow and disintegrate, man reaches, stumbles forward, painfully, mistakenly sometimes.

b) Worried because __________ do not work out; hungry for security and yet sensing its disappearance from the earth.

c) And her plump face was tight against the movement, and her head __________ sharply because her neck muscles were tight.

d) She dropped her weapon on the ground, and Tom, with __________ care, picked it up and put it back in the car.

e) The __________ man rubbed his forehead with a knuckle, and a line of dirt peeled off.

2. Complete each sentence with a word from the list.

spatula	buzzard	flush	piston	clod

a) A pie lifter won't do it; you're going to need a proper __________.

b) Jeremy spotted the book his sister had been reading because it was not __________ with the other books on the shelf.

c) The truck's rear wheels spun, throwing up dirt, one __________ of which struck a second floor window.

d) The __________ peeking in at her through her window hinted to Beverly that it might be time to clean out the fridge.

e) The loud banging from the engine seemed to Susan must be a __________ misfiring.

NAME: ______________________________

Chapters Fourteen to Sixteen

Answer each question with a complete sentence.

1. Western land owners are fighting the widening government, labor unity and strikes. What's the real problem?

2. After protesting to Al about selling a whole loaf of bread for ten cents, Mae sells two nickel-a-piece candies for a penny. Why do you think she did that?

3. Why did Casy say he had been so quiet?

4. Tom isn't thinking about anything but the task immediately in front of him. Why?

5. Why did Ma want the family to camp where there was shade and water?

6. When Tom was told he'd have to pay another fifty cents to stay at the campground, what did he decide to do?

You are a cook in a diner along Route 66. You know from people returning from California just how bad the job situation is. Write a journal entry in which you try to convince a family heading west, to change their plans and look for work somewhere else.

NAME: ______________________________

Chapters Seventeen to Nineteen

Vocabulary

encampment
puckering
decorous
tarpaulin
timid
gunny
illuminated
accumulation
jabbering
cemented
snorting
drowsed
courtesies

Across

1. A protective covering of canvas or other material waterproofed with tar, paint, or wax.
4. Considerate acts.
5. A place with temporary accommodations consisting of huts or tents.
7. To supply or brighten with light.
8. In keeping with good taste and propriety.
10. Talking rapidly, indistinctly, incoherently, or nonsensically.
11. Made from jute or burlap.
12. Forcing the breath violently through the nostrils with a loud, harsh sound.
13. Was half-asleep.

Down

2. Gathered into small wrinkles or folds.
3. Growth by continuous additions.
6. Lacking in self-assurance, courage, or bravery.
9. United permanently.

After You Read

NAME: ______________________________

Chapters Seventeen to Nineteen

1. Complete the paragraphs by filling in each blank with the correct word from the chapters.

A certain physical pattern is needed for the ____________ (a) of a world—water, a river bank, a stream, a spring, or even a faucet ____________ (b). And there is needed enough flat land to pitch the tents, a little brush or wood to build the fires. If there is a garbage dump not too far off, all the better; for there can be found ____________ (c)—stove tops, a curved fender to shelter the fire, and cans to cook in and to eat from.

The men ____________ (d) off their pants, peeled their shirts, and waded out. The dust coated their legs to the knee, their feet were pale and soft with sweat. They settled lazily into the water and washed listlessly at their flanks. Sun-bitten, they were, a father and a boy. They ____________ (e) and groaned with the water.

Now the high voice broke into hysteria, the ____________ (f) screams of a hyena, the thudding became louder. Voices cracked and broke, and then the whole chorus fell to a sobbing, grunting undertone, and the slap of flesh and the ____________ (g) on the earth; and the sobbing changed to a little whining, like that of a litter of puppies at a food dish.

Now farming became ____________ (h), and the owners followed Rome, although they did not know it. They ____________ (i) slaves, although they did not call them slaves: Chinese, Japanese, Mexicans, Filipinos. They live on rice and beans, the business men said. They don't need much. They wouldn't know what to do with good wages. Why, look how they live. Why, look what they eat. And if they get funny—____________ (j) them.

NAME: ______________________________

After You Read

Chapters Seventeen to Nineteen

Answer each question with a complete sentence.

1. As families moved westward, what changed about their stopping places each night?

2. What were the punishments for breaking the rules of the encampments?

3. Why did Noah leave the family?

4. Why didn't Ma want the Jehovites to hold a prayer meeting for Granma in their tent?

5. Why did Ma not want the officer looking in the back of the truck?

6. What were the landowners most afraid of when the farmers began to come to California?

Imagine that you are part of a family moving west along with the others. Write a journal entry describing your first night in one of the large encampments that form every evening.

Before You Read

NAME: ____________________

Chapters Twenty to Twenty-one

Answer the questions in complete sentences.

1. If you had no money, no food and couldn't get work, what would you do for food?

___

___

___

2. Would you be more or less likely to trust other people, if you were in the Joads' position?

___

___

___

Vocabulary

Synonyms are words with similar meanings. Use the context of the sentences below to help you choose the best synonym for the underlined word in each sentence. If you cannot determine the meaning from the context, consult a dictionary.

1. Jane **snooped** around the house until she found where the presents were.
   a) pried **b)** looked **c)** hid **d)** concealed
2. No one wanted to play with Jeremy because of the way he was **comporting** himself.
   a) misbehaving **b)** disputing **c)** bearing **d)** misconducting
3. Jules's attempts to make things up to Joanne were met with **resentment**.
   a) affection **b)** bitterness **c)** liking **d)** pleasure
4. Due to his **unkempt** appearance, John's mom made him clean up before eating dinner.
   a) clean **b)** spotless **c)** pure **d)** dishevelled
5. None of the paintings were classical; they all dated from a later, **degenerate** period.
   a) commendable **b)** degraded **c)** moral **d)** worthy
6. The pump operated **mechanically** without any need for supervision.
   a) automatically **b)** erratically **c)** unevenly **d)** irregularly

NAME: ______________________________

Chapters Twenty to Twenty-one

1. Put a check mark (✓) next to the answer that is most correct.

a) What happened after Ma Joad gave the children some of the food?

- ◯ **A** A woman came by to thank her.
- ◯ **B** The children said they'd be back next day.
- ◯ **C** A woman came by to scold her for feeding her child.
- ◯ **D** The children offered to do chores for more food.

b) What did Floyd say would happen if the workers organized?

- ◯ **A** They'd get better wages.
- ◯ **B** The owners would just get someone else.
- ◯ **C** The organizers would get arrested.
- ◯ **D** The crops wouldn't get harvested.

c) What was Floyd's advice to Tom for when the police come around?

- ◯ **A** Pretend to be dumb.
- ◯ **B** Avoid them.
- ◯ **C** Fight them.
- ◯ **D** Be as nice to them as he can.

d) What did Ma Joad say she wanted most when told about the government camp?

- ◯ **A** A bath.
- ◯ **B** To go to a dance.
- ◯ **C** A safe place for her family.
- ◯ **D** A washtub.

e) What did the landowners do to get rid of most of their competition?

- ◯ **A** Bought canneries to drive the price of fruit down.
- ◯ **B** Hired more workers so that the smaller farmers couldn't hire enough men to harvest their crop.
- ◯ **C** Had the police stop everyone from working the smaller farmers' land.
- ◯ **D** All of the above.

After You Read

NAME: ______________________

Chapters Twenty to Twenty-one

Answer each question with a complete sentence.

1. What upset Ma Joad most about Granma dying?

2. What was wrong with the "Mayor" of Hooverville?

3. Besides getting arrested, what else would happen to someone trying to organize the workers for better pay?

4. Why did the landowners put out so many hand bills?

5. What did the cop threaten, if the men didn't go to work in Tulare County?

6. Why do you think Casy covered for Tom when the police came back?

Write a journal entry detailing what you might do to get better wages for work, if you were in the same situation as the Joads.

NAME: ________________________

Chapters Twenty-two to Twenty-three

Answer the questions in complete sentences.

1. Do you think the Joads will find a safe place at the government camp? Why or why not?

____

____

____

2. What will determine the length of the Joad's stay in the government camp?

____

____

____

Vocabulary

Circle the correct word that matches the meaning of the underlined word.

1. "Well, s'pose a fella is jus' mean, or drunk an' **quarrelsome**. What then?"

a) conciliatory **b)** confrontational **c)** morose **d)** depressed

2. Ruthie came **wriggling** out like a snake, her hair down over her eyes and her dress wrinkled and twisted.

a) sliding **b)** crawling **c)** squirming **d)** walking

3. Citizens, angered at red **agitators**, burn squatters' camp.

a) protesters **b)** revellers **c)** settlers **d)** anarchists

4. "Lected **unanimous**," she said.

a) undecided **b)** undisputed **c)** opposed **d)** individual

5. Jessie's voice became almost **reverential**.

a) quiet **b)** awed **c)** disdainful **d)** mirthful

6. "I says I was gonna play," she said **triumphantly**.

a) modestly **b)** teasingly **c)** exultantly **d)** mirthfully

After You Read

NAME: ____________________

Chapters Twenty-two to Twenty-three

Fill in each blank with the correct word from the chapters.

a) The whole camp ____________ and snorted.

b) But a little movement started among the ____________.

c) His father opened the barn and passed out two ____________ and three shovels.

d) Her eyes rolled up, her shoulders and arms ____________ loosely at her side, and a string of thick ropy saliva ran from the corner of her mouth.

e) Playing a reel and tapping out the tune, and the big deep strings of the guitar beating like a heart, and the harmonica's sharp chords and the ____________ and squeal of the fiddle.

Vocabulary

Complete each sentence with a word from the list.

headband	watchman	fistfuls	raddled	sugared	gingham

a) ____________, one feather.

b) She turned back to the ____________ little woman.

c) The ____________ stepped up on the running board.

d) She wore a great apron, made from a cotton bag, over her ____________ dress, and men's brown oxfords were on her feet.

e) Ma turned from the cornmeal she was measuring in ____________.

f) They filled their plates, poured bacon gravy over the biscuits, and ____________ their coffee.

NAME: ______________________

Chapters Twenty-two to Twenty-three

Answer each question with a complete sentence.

1. What happened just as Tom was pulling up to the government camp entrance?

____

____

____

2. What happened to Tom the first morning at the government camp?

____

____

3. When Jim Rawley came to visit Ma Joad, what most reassured her about him?

____

____

4. Why was Rose of Sharon afraid she was going to miscarry ('drop the baby')?

____

____

5. What caused Mrs. Sandry's fit?

____

____

6. Why do you think the migrant farmers were so hungry for amusement?

____

____

____

What kind of living conditions would you be willing to put up with in exchange for good paying work? Suppose someone offered you good work, but you had to leave the government camp to do it. Write an imagined conversation between yourself and someone making you such an offer.

NAME: ______________________

Chapters Twenty-four to Twenty-five

Answer the questions in complete sentences.

1. Do you think that violence would be justified to prevent the starvation of the migrant workers and their families?

2. Why aren't there more government camps?

Vocabulary **Write a complete sentence using the following words. Make sure that the meaning of each word is clear in your sentence.**

Friction ______________________

Engagingly ______________________

Bristled ______________________

Vibrant ______________________

Fruitfulness ______________________

Cultivators ______________________

Denunciation ______________________

Symbolize ______________________

Irrigation ______________________

NAME: ______________________

Chapters Twenty-four to Twenty-five

1. Complete the paragraphs by filling in each blank with the correct word from the chapters.

At the big open-air dance platform a ____(a)____ was busy. Every bit of electric wire had been ____(b)____. The city dump had been visited for wire, every tool box had ____(c)____ friction tape. And now the patched, ____(d)____ wire was strung out to the dance floor, with bottle necks as ____(e)____. This night the floor would be ____(f)____ for the first time. By six o'clock the men were back from work or from looking for work, and a new wave of ____(g)____ started. By seven, dinners were over, men had on their best clothes: freshly washed ____(h)____, clean blue shirts, sometimes the decent blacks. The girls were ready in their print dresses, ____(i)____ and clean, their hair braided and ____(j)____. The worried women watched the families and cleaned up the evening dishes. On the ____(k)____ the string band ____(l)____, surrounded by a double wall of children. The people were ____(m)____ and excited.

2. Choose the most appropriate answer for each of the following:

a) Who was the entertainment chairman?

- ◯ **A** Jim Casy
- ◯ **B** Willie Eaton
- ◯ **C** Tom Joad
- ◯ **D** Ezra Huston

b) How did the troublemakers get in?

- ◯ **A** Through the front gate.
- ◯ **B** Over the fence.
- ◯ **C** None got in.
- ◯ **D** Guests of Ezra Huston.

c) Rose of Sharon would only go to the dance if...

- ◯ **A** someone would dance with her.
- ◯ **B** Ma would sit with her.
- ◯ **C** Connie came back.
- ◯ **D** she didn't have to dance.

d) What happened to the unsold fruit?

- ◯ **A** It was canned.
- ◯ **B** It was given away.
- ◯ **C** It was sold for a loss.
- ◯ **D** It was destroyed.

After You Read

NAME: ____________________

Chapters Twenty-four to Twenty-five

Answer each question with a complete sentence.

1. What was the plan to keep troublemakers from starting a fight at the dance?

2. Why didn't Rose of Sharon want to go to the dance?

3. What did the chairman of the Entertainment Committee want Tom for?

4. Why didn't Pa and Uncle John get work?

5. Why didn't the children of the migrant workers like the schools in California?

6. How did the troublemakers make it past the gate into the camp?

Write a journal entry in which you are a farmer faced with the choice of destroying your crop or giving it away to the starving migrants.

NAME: ______________________

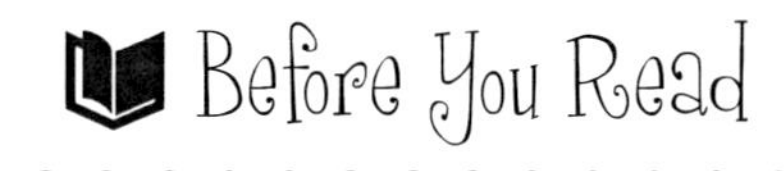

Chapters Twenty-six to Twenty-seven

Answer the questions in a complete sentence.

1. Would you rather be comfortable and hungry or uncomfortable but with enough food to eat? Why?

2. Would you strike for a living wage? Why or why not?

Vocabulary

In each of the following sets of words, underline the one word which does not belong. Then write a sentence explaining why it does not fit.

1. **a)** fragment **b)** shard **c)** splinter **d)** join

2. **a)** coughed **b)** spluttered **c)** enunciate **d)** stuttered

3. **a)** happily **b)** forlornly **c)** miserably **d)** dejectedly

4. **a)** stubble **b)** straw **c)** growth **d)** smooth

5. **a)** stifled **b)** bare **c)** oppressed **d)** smothered

After You Read

NAME: ______________________________

Chapters Twenty-six to Twenty-seven

1. Put a check mark (✓) next to the answer that is most correct.

a) What did Ma say when Pa threatened her with a stick?

- ◯ **A** Told him he could beat her if he wanted.
- ◯ **B** Threatened him right back.
- ◯ **C** Told him he had to decide what to do.
- ◯ **D** Told him what they were going to do.

b) What was the problem with the car the morning the Joads left the government camp?

- ◯ **A** There was no gas.
- ◯ **B** The starter was broken.
- ◯ **C** It had a flat.
- ◯ **D** The battery was dead.

c) Why was it hard to get into the farm to pick peaches?

- ◯ **A** The road was out.
- ◯ **B** There were too many other people working.
- ◯ **C** There was a strike by other workers.
- ◯ **D** The wages were very low.

d) What happened when Tom brought his first box full of peaches?

- ◯ **A** It was rejected because the peaches were bruised.
- ◯ **B** He was paid a nickel.
- ◯ **C** He was credited a nickel.
- ◯ **D** He was told the box wasn't full, yet.

e) Why did the cops think Casy was leading the strike?

- ◯ **A** Because he said he was.
- ◯ **B** Because he talked the most.
- ◯ **C** Because the strike was his idea.
- ◯ **D** No one knew why.

NAME: ______________________________

Chapters Twenty-six to Twenty-seven

Answer each question with a complete sentence.

1. Why did the Joads have to leave the government camp?

____

____

2. What did Al have to do to get the car started the morning the Joads left the government camp?

____

____

____

3. What did Ma decide to do when she heard about the fight Tom got in?

____

____

____

4. Why was Rose of Sharon so upset to learn that Tom killed someone?

____

____

5. How did the Joads get Tom out of the camp without him being spotted?

____

____

6. How did Tom plan to stay out of sight when the rest were picking cotton?

____

____

Write a journal entry in which you tell what happened when you told the pickers that their wages would be cut in half after the strike was broken.

NAME: ______________________

Chapters Twenty-eight to Thirty

Answer the questions in complete sentences.

1. What do you think will happen to the Joads when there are no more crops to be harvested in California?

____

____

____

2. How do you think Casy's death will affect Tom's view of the world?

____

____

____

Vocabulary

Choose a word from the list that means the same as the underlined word.

pitched	**screeched**	**lusterless**	**utensils**
floundered	**scooped**	**elaborate**	**mysteriously**

1. James **stumbled** around in the dark, looking for the light switch.
2. The owl **shrieked** when it spotted the mouse scuttling across the barn floor.
3. The lace shawl had an **intricate** design of trees in bloom on its back.
4. Jade **gathered** as many blueberries in her apron as she could.
5. With a grunt of disgust, David **flung** the dirty sock as far away from him as he could.
6. As usual, Crystal had the job of putting the **silverware** out for dinner.
7. "You'll have to wait 'til Sunday," Jared whispered, **cryptically**.
8. With a heavy sigh, Katelyn contemplated the drab, **dingy** room she'd be staying in.

NAME: ______________________

After You Read

Chapters Twenty-eight to Thirty

1. Circle T if the statement is TRUE or F if it is FALSE.

T F **a)** Winfield got in a fight and told about his brother killing two people.

T F **b)** Tom told Ma Joad that he had decided to follow in Casy's footsteps.

T F **c)** The last cotton field was picked completely by 11 a.m.

T F **d)** It started to rain before all the cotton in the last field was picked.

T F **e)** The bank that the men made to stop the creek flooding the camp worked.

T F **f)** Rose of Sharon had a bad cold when she went into labor.

2. Number the events from 1 to 6 in the order they occurred in these chapters.

☐ **a)** Al and Aggie announce that they are getting married.

☐ **b)** Rose of Sharon's baby is stillborn.

☐ **c)** Ma Joad tells Tom about people finding out that he killed two people.

☐ **d)** The farmers build a bank to stop the creek flooding the camp.

☐ **e)** The family picks the last field of cotton.

☐ **f)** Tom leaves the family.

After You Read

NAME: ______________________________

Chapters Twenty-eight to Thirty

Answer each question with a complete sentence.

1. What did Winfield want Ma Joad to do about Ruthie telling about Tom being a murderer?

___

___

2. What did Tom do while he was alone, hiding in the cave?

___

___

3. What was the reaction to Al and Aggie's engagement announcement?

___

___

4. Why did the townspeople start to fear the people coming into town to beg for food?

___

___

5. What happened at the end of the work to build a bank to stop the creek flooding the camp?

___

___

6. Why did Rose of Sharon smile when she fed the starving man from her own breast milk?

___

___

Write a journal entry in which you describe how the remainder of the Joad family survives the winter in California.

Chapters 1 to 5

Dialogue

In the beginning of the novel, the crops fail again. We know the soil is too poor to grow a good crop. Chapter five presents us with the crisis that drives the Joad family and so many others off the land and on to California.

Place yourself in the role of a tenant farmer with a family when a representative of the landowner comes to tell you that you have to leave the farm immediately.

Write the dialogue that would follow as if it were an interview with you asking the questions and the other answering them.

Chapters 6 to 17

Handbills

The notion of going to California comes from handbills telling about many jobs, good wages, and great living conditions to be had out west.

This section covers the move west, during which the Joads come to doubt the sincerity of the authors of the advertisements.

Make up one of these handbills. Try to make it as enticing as possible, keeping in mind the point-of-view of the tenant farmer in the Dust Bowl. Try to make it as authentic as possible (i.e. use the language of the period, use pictures that would not have been out of place in the 1930s in Middle America, etc.).

Chapters 18 to 25

Characterizing the Land

The land in Oklahoma was worked steadily and lovingly by farmers who didn't own it. Despite that, it became less and less fertile, largely because mistakes were made in what was grown and how.

In contrast, the land in California is rich and the crops grown there thrive. There are scientists who make sure that the soil stays rich and that the crops themselves stay healthy and free from parasites. Yet the land is worked by people who do not care for it.

Steinbeck's philosophy concerns the tragedy of the commercialization of farming. The soil, the land in *The Grapes of Wrath* is almost a character in itself.

Write an essay, describing the land as if it were a person. What does it look like, act like? What would it say for itself? How does this change over the course of the story? How would it feel about its treatment by the various groups in the story?

Chapters 26 to 27

A Police Report

The workers striking at the orchard when the Joads show up are angry because they were expected to work for less than what would feed them and their families.

This anger and the determination of the landowners and the police to prevent group action led to the murder of two men: Jim Casy and Casy's killer.

Imagine that you are a police officer who was not present for any of the events, but now has to investigate what happened. Write up a police report about the incident. Provide as much detail about what happened, beginning with the original unrest and ending with the return to the wage that caused the upset in the beginning.

Chapters 28 to 29

Write a Scene

When Tom leaves, he is on the run for the murder of the man who killed Jim Casy. Steinbeck leaves us wondering what will happen to him. Being as he intends to follow in Casy's footsteps, as he has done all along, there's a good chance he might get captured.

Write a scene in which Tom Joad is on trial for the murder of the man with the pick handle. Include Tom's testimony as to what happened and his defense of his actions when cross-examined by the prosecuting attorney.

Chapter 30

Newspaper Article

Besides Tom, there are others in the story whose fate we are left to speculate about. Write a newspaper article telling about the fates of the characters who are alive at the end of the story.

NAME: ______________________________

Word Search Puzzle

Find the following words from the story. The words are written horizontally, vertically, diagonally, and some are written backwards.

panoramically	**headband**	**heifer**	**splattering**
puckering	**fistfuls**	**lusterless**	**paling**
degenerate	**drone**	**anlage**	**babbitt**
bristled	**cannery**	**tannic**	**sheaf**
exhortation	**vagrant**	**truculent**	**boxcar**

d	j	e	l	g	h	d	s	r	b	i	o	h	b	s	r	a	w	a	v	w	a
f	f	g	r	b	t	a	s	f	y	s	q	d	w	a	m	c	i	s	b	z	l
h	v	h	f	f	g	b	e	b	g	d	x	s	r	v	p	f	l	f	p	a	o
y	o	j	i	w	i	j	l	s	q	v	q	e	f	y	i	r	i	g	i	f	i
w	i	e	u	h	u	y	r	h	u	g	e	f	s	n	h	q	k	t	k	t	k
j	j	d	g	y	q	w	e	i	p	l	t	b	h	k	b	b	h	n	h	h	u
u	h	u	p	p	l	n	t	r	u	c	u	l	e	n	t	v	b	x	j	f	j
e	r	h	o	a	k	k	s	l	u	a	b	c	a	b	e	a	q	i	t	f	h
a	r	i	e	l	h	i	u	d	l	c	c	s	f	v	q	m	w	j	g	j	b
f	e	b	r	i	s	t	l	e	d	b	q	e	i	g	s	i	f	o	q	h	g
g	y	a	i	n	f	p	d	g	a	h	x	d	o	v	i	f	v	a	e	d	g
r	h	c	u	g	a	e	a	e	x	h	o	r	t	a	t	i	o	n	z	a	r
o	a	s	j	a	t	h	r	n	l	t	q	o	a	g	y	s	t	l	h	k	e
u	b	c	t	g	j	f	m	e	o	f	e	n	n	r	m	t	c	a	e	s	s
g	t	n	x	k	t	t	r	r	p	r	r	e	n	a	q	f	a	g	a	a	z
m	q	b	w	o	g	n	i	a	o	o	a	o	i	n	r	u	n	e	d	x	c
k	w	c	b	a	b	b	i	t	t	n	g	m	c	t	y	l	n	l	b	b	g
s	r	o	b	g	a	o	k	e	y	f	s	r	i	a	h	s	e	a	a	t	j
t	y	l	y	f	s	l	n	s	c	a	l	p	u	c	k	e	r	i	n	g	m
w	u	h	r	s	d	f	y	a	s	v	l	s	l	v	a	u	y	v	d	j	l
r	q	u	d	h	g	g	d	h	d	h	y	c	g	a	a	l	l	n	q	d	o
v	e	m	g	k	n	s	h	v	g	t	n	b	b	y	t	n	l	i	r	q	i
e	e	s	u	o	f	e	l	n	m	w	v	h	i	b	p	t	j	y	i	a	u
s	u	q	j	u	u	v	i	j	k	h	w	u	a	n	u	k	e	l	l	f	h
d	u	f	u	b	h	n	u	i	g	s	e	k	a	j	n	l	u	r	k	j	y
u	h	u	e	f	e	h	h	y	y	a	f	o	g	i	b	e	q	u	i	i	e
l	r	k	y	k	d	d	g	e	u	v	o	l	r	f	r	a	a	e	q	n	d
i	d	l	h	n	l	a	r	d	h	m	i	a	e	g	q	p	w	d	a	l	g

Comprehension Quiz

28

Answer each question in a complete sentence.

1. What was Jim Casy doing when we first met him in the novel? 2

2. When the company men are evicting the farmers, what reason do they give? 2

3. Why does Jim Casy say he wants to go West with the Joads? 2

4. Why do the Joads decide to help the Wilsons with their car? 2

5. After Al told Mae to give the man a whole loaf of bread, what did she do? 2

6. How did Tom stop the bleeding on his hand when he cut it? 2

7. What advice did Tom give to the one-eyed man? 3

SUBTOTAL: /15

NAME: ______________________

Comprehension Quiz

8. Why did Noah say he wasn't going with the rest of the family anymore? 2

9. Why did Jim Casy offer to take the blame for assaulting the police officer? 2

10. Why was Rose of Sharon afraid she was going to miscarry? 2

11. What did Black Hat suggest as the solution to the problem of the lower and lower wages? 2

12. The man who ran the store wouldn't give Ma credit for some sugar. What did he do instead? 2

13. What started the fight that led to Ruthie telling about Tom being a murderer? 1

14. Chapter One and Chapter Twenty-Nine mirror each other in many ways. Besides too much versus too little rain, what other main difference is there between the two chapters? 2

SUBTOTAL: /13

1. Answers will vary.

2. Answers will vary.

Vocabulary

1. proboscis
2. sheathing
3. declivity
4. chambray
5. parapet
6. fallow
7. germinate
8. emulsion

11

1.

a) ✓ D

b) ✓ C

c) ✓ D

d) ✓ B

e) ✓ A

12

---

1. The crops grew quickly and then wilted (because of the lack of more rain).

2. The Trucker won't drink because "A guy can't drink liquor all the time and study like I'm goin' to."

3. Three grains of wild oats are moved and planted by the turtle. Answers will vary but should say something about the tenacity of the turtle, the cats and the people in the story.

4. The inmate wanted to return because the prison had better food, electricity, good beds, books and he didn't have to think about what to do next.

5. Crop rotation and letting land lie fallow would have allowed the soil to replenish itself.

13

---

1. Answers will vary.

2. Answers will vary.

Vocabulary

1. D
2. H
3. B
4. C
5. J
6. F
7. A
8. E
9. G
10. I

14

1.

a) F
b) T
c) F
d) T
e) T
f) T

2.

a) 4
b) 6
c) 3
d) 2
e) 1
f) 5

15

---

1. Tom's Ma knew Pretty Boy Floyd and his mom and was afraid that what happened to him might have happened to her son.

2. Tom knew his family was gone from the farm or dead because the pig gate was left open and it never would have been, if they'd been there.

3. Tom would kill the man Turnbull in the same circumstances, feeling he was justified in doing so the first time.

4. The farmers are desperate to buy and the salesmen know they can get outrageous prices on any car, so the cheaper the car is, the more profit they make.

5. Answers will vary.

6. Answers will vary.

16

EZ✓

17

1. Answers will vary.

2. Answers will vary.

Vocabulary

1. talcum

2. mattock

3. provocatively

4. vacant

5. wizened

6. gulch

7. whisked

8. tributary

18

1.

a) pregnant

b) swamp

c) outcropping

d) junk

e) licorice

2.

a) chattering

b) puckered

c) scampered

d) transgression

e) heifer

19

1. The Joad men kill, butcher and salt two pigs.

2. If they should ever meet his folks, Muley wanted the Joads to tell them he was alright.

3. First came boys from the town, and then came cats, then bats, mice, weasels and finally owls.

4. Al was most worried about crossing the mountains because the car was overloaded and the engine might burn out.

5. Tom wasn't worried because no one would know he'd left the state if he didn't commit any crimes.

6. Grampa Joad died because he couldn't leave the land he was born and raised on.

20

1. Answers will vary.

2. Answers will vary.

Vocabulary

1. dungarees

2. corrugated

3. coroner

4. contractor

5. streamlined

6. bewildered

7. gasket

8. proprietor

21

1.

a) philosophies

b) formulas

c) jiggled

d) elaborate

e) one-eyed

2.

a) spatula

b) flush

c) clod

d) buzzard

e) piston

22

1. The real problem is the hunger of hundreds of thousands of former farmers and their families who no longer have work or homes.

2. Answers will vary.

3. Casy was quiet because he was lusting after flesh and thinking that, if he weren't a preacher any more, he should get married.

4. Answers may vary, but should mention that Tom is worried about what might happen in California, considering how many people are moving west looking for work.

5. Ma wanted to camp where there was water and shade because of Granma, who has been ranting at Grampa, who died a few days previous.

6. Tom decided that he, Casy and Uncle John would take the car down the road and wait for the others to come by in the morning.

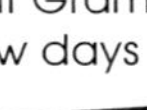

Vocabulary

Across

1. tarpaulin
4. courtesies
5. encampment
7. illuminated
8. decorous
10. jabbering
11. gunny
12. snorting
13. drowsed

Down

2. puckering
3. accumulation
6. timid
9. cemented

23

1.

a) building

b) unguarded

c) equipment

d) shucked

e) grunted

f) gabbling

g) thuddings

h) industry

i) imported

j) deport

24

1. The stopping places of the families moving westward became little communities that offered protection and the security and comfort of rules.

2. The only punishments for violation of the encampment rules were banishment or violence.

3. Noah stayed behind because the family didn't really care for him.

4. She couldn't stand the thought of the Jehovites howling and jumping.

5. Ma didn't want the officer looking in the back of the truck because Granma had died and she didn't want the family stopped before they got through the desert.

6. The landowners were most afraid that the farmers will just take the land the way their forbearers just took it from the Mexicans.

25

1. Answers will vary.

2. Answers will vary.

Vocabulary

1. a

2. c

3. b

4. d

5. b

6. a

26

1.

a) ✓ **C**

b) ✓ **C**

c) ✓ **A**

d) ✓ **D**

e) ✓ **A**

27

1. Ma Joad regretted not being able to give Granma a nice funeral, like she would've wanted.

2. The cops beat on him so much he became "bull-simple".

3. Labor organizers could get blacklisted, meaning no one would ever hire them.

4. The more people who showed up to work the fields, the less money they'd have to pay them.

5. The cop said that the camp might be cleaned by men with pick handles.

6. Answers will vary.

28

EZ✓

EZ✔

29

1. Answers will vary.

2. Answers will vary.

Vocabulary

1. b

2. c

3. a

4. b

5. b

6. c

30

1.

a) buzzed

b) bedclothes

c) picks

d) flopped

e) skirl

2.

a) headband

b) raddled

c) watchman

d) gingham

e) fistfuls

f) sugared

31

1. Tom drove over a speed bump he didn't know was there.

2. Tom was offered breakfast and a job his first morning at the camp.

3. The frayed seams on Jim Rawley's white coat.

4. Rose of Sharon was afraid she was going to miscarry because she 'hug danced'.

5. Answers may vary, but should mention either that she is unwell or crazy or that Ma Joad threatened her.

6. Answers will vary.

32

1. Answers will vary.

2. Answers will vary.

Vocabulary Answers will vary.

33

1.

a) committee

b) requisitioned

c) contributed
d) spliced

e) insulators
f) lighted

g) bathing

h) overalls

i) stretched

j) ribboned

k) platform
l) practiced

m) intent

2.

a) ✔ **B** **b)** ✔ **A**

c) ✔ **D** **d)** ✔ **D**

34

1. To stop trouble at the dance, a committee put men at the gate, patrolling the fence and on the dance floor to escort troublemakers out of the camp without hurting them.

2. Rose of Sharon didn't want to go to the dance because she didn't want anyone looking at her.

3. The chairman of the Entertainment Committee wanted Tom to help stop trouble at the dance by watching out for troublemakers trying to start a fight.

4. Pa and Uncle John didn't get work because they were expected to work for 20 cents an hour.

5. The children didn't like the schools because they were picked on and got into fights because of their ragged appearance.

6. The troublemakers said that Jackson from Unit 4 asked them to come.

1. Answers will vary.

2. Answers will vary.

Vocabulary
Reasons will vary.

1. d

2. c

3. a

4. d

5. b

35

1.

a) ✓ B

b) ✓ C

c) ✓ C

d) ✓ A

e) ✓ B

36

---

1. The Joads had to leave the government camp because there was no work and the food was running out.

2. Al had to crank start the engine the morning the Joads left the government camp because the battery was flat.

3. Ma decided to hide Tom and get the family out of the peach orchard that evening.

4. Rose of Sharon was upset because she feared Tom's crime would cause her to lose her baby.

5. Tom was smuggled out between the two mattresses on the back of the car.

6. Tom decided to hide in some heavy brush by the road until his face healed, relying on Ma to bring him meals.

37

---

1. Answers will vary.

2. Answers will vary.

Vocabulary

1. floundered

2. screeched

3. elaborate

4. scooped

5. pitched

6. utensils

7. mysteriously

8. lusterless

38

1.

a) F

b) T

c) T

d) F

e) F

f) T

2.

a) 3

b) 6

c) 1

d) 5

e) 4

f) 2

39

---

1. Winfield wanted Ma Joad to beat Ruthie for telling and getting Tom in trouble.

2. When Tom was alone in the cave, he thought about things Casy said.

3. Both families got together to celebrate with coffee and pancakes.

4. Answers may vary, but should mention fear of the beggars' desperation.

5. At the end of the work, a cotton tree uprooted and tore out a section of the bank, causing the flooding of the camp.

6. Answers will vary.

40

EZ✓

Word Search Puzzle

d	j	e	l	g	h	d	s	r	b	i	o	h	b	s	r	a	w	a	v	w	a
f	f	g	r	b	t	a	s	f	y	s	q	d	w	a	m	c	i	s	b	z	l
h	v	h	f	f	g	b	e	b	g	d	x	s	r	v	p	f	l	f	p	a	o
y	o	j	i	w	i	j	l	s	q	v	q	e	f	y	i	r	i	g	i	f	i
w	i	e	u	h	u	y	r	h	u	g	e	f	s	n	h	q	k	t	k	t	k
j	j	d	g	y	q	w	e	i	p	l	t	b	h	k	b	b	h	n	h	h	u
u	h	u	p	p	l	n	t	r	u	c	u	l	e	n	t	v	b	x	j	f	j
e	r	h	o	a	k	k	s	l	u	a	b	c	a	b	e	a	q	i	t	f	h
a	r	i	e	l	h	i	u	d	l	c	c	s	f	v	q	m	w	j	g	j	b
f	e	b	r	i	s	t	l	e	d	b	q	e	i	g	s	i	f	o	q	h	g
g	y	a	i	n	f	p	d	g	a	h	x	d	o	v	i	f	v	a	e	d	g
r	h	c	u	g	a	e	a	e	x	h	o	r	t	a	t	i	o	n	z	a	r
o	a	s	j	a	t	h	r	n	l	t	q	o	a	g	y	s	t	l	h	k	e
u	b	c	t	g	j	f	m	e	o	f	e	n	n	r	m	t	c	a	e	s	s
g	t	n	x	k	t	t	r	r	p	r	r	e	n	a	q	f	a	g	a	a	z
m	q	b	w	o	g	n	i	a	o	o	a	o	i	n	r	u	n	e	d	x	c
k	w	c	b	a	b	b	i	t	t	n	g	m	c	t	y	l	n	l	b	b	g
s	r	o	b	g	a	o	k	e	y	f	s	r	i	a	h	s	e	a	a	t	j
t	y	l	y	f	s	l	n	s	c	a	l	p	u	c	k	e	r	i	n	g	m
w	u	h	r	s	d	f	y	a	s	v	l	s	l	v	a	u	y	v	d	j	l
r	q	u	d	h	g	g	d	h	d	h	y	c	g	a	a	l	l	n	q	d	o
v	e	m	g	k	n	s	h	v	g	t	n	b	b	y	t	n	l	i	r	q	i
e	e	s	u	o	f	e	l	n	m	w	v	h	i	b	p	t	j	y	i	a	u
s	u	q	j	u	u	v	i	j	k	h	w	u	a	n	u	k	e	l	l	f	h
d	u	f	u	b	h	n	u	i	g	s	e	k	a	j	n	l	u	r	k	j	y
u	h	u	e	f	e	h	h	y	y	a	f	o	g	i	b	e	q	u	i	i	e
l	r	k	y	k	d	d	g	e	u	v	o	l	r	f	r	a	a	e	q	n	d
i	d	l	h	n	l	a	r	d	h	m	i	a	e	g	q	p	w	d	a	l	g

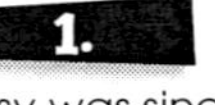

1. Jim Casy was singing a song about Jesus to the tune of "Yes, Sir, That's My Baby."

2. The company men blame the banks and their need for money.

3. Casy wants to be with people just living their lives, because he has discovered that the good things in life are holy.

4. The Joads help the Wilsons because they helped bury Grampa and that makes them almost family.

5. Mae gave the man the loaf of bread and sold two pieces of nickel candy for a single penny.

6. Tom urinated onto the dirt and used the resulting mud to cover the cut.

7. Tom told the one-eyed man to stop complaining, clean himself up and cover his empty eye socket.

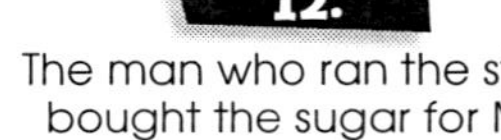

8. Noah couldn't make himself leave the river and wanted to walk beside it and fish.

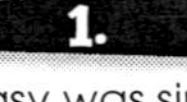

9. Casy took the blame because if Tom were arrested, they'd know he broke parole by leaving Oklahoma.

10. Rose of Sharon was afraid she was going to miscarry because a religious woman at the government camp told her that's what happened to pregnant women who close danced or acted in plays.

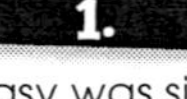

11. Black Hat suggested that all the workers get together and kill all the landowners.

12. The man who ran the store bought the sugar for Ma and asked her to repay him the next day.

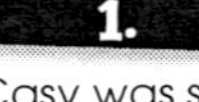

13. The fight started because some kid stole Ruthie's Cracker Jack.

14. In Chapter One, each farmer stands alone while his family looks on anxiously, while in Chapter Twenty-Nine, the farmers stand together and talk about the crisis.

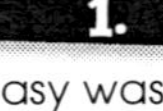
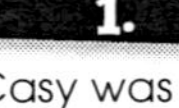

The Structure of *The Grapes of Wrath*

Determine the parallels between the two types of chapters and identify the conflict, antagonist, protagonist, climax, falling action, point of view, theme, setting, and conclusion for each.

Expositional Chapters	Narrative Chapters
Ch. 1:	Ch. 2:
Ch. 3:	Ch. 4:
Ch. 5:	Ch. 6:
Ch. 7	Ch. 8:
Ch. 9:	Ch. 10:
Ch. 11:	
Ch. 12:	Ch. 13:
Ch. 14:	
Ch. 15:	Ch. 16:
Ch. 17:	Ch. 18:
Ch. 19:	Ch. 20:
Ch. 21:	Ch. 22:
Ch. 23:	Ch. 24:
Ch. 25:	Ch. 26:
Ch. 27:	Ch. 28:
Ch. 29:	Ch. 30:

Character Analysis: Tom Joad

Describe how Tom Joad's views on life and justice had changed after each of the following events in the novel.

Time in prison for murder

Initial conversation with Jim Casy

Family's Eviction

The Journey to California

Life in California until Casy's Death

Time alone in the cave, while hiding

Themes

Discuss the themes of the novel — in particular how they are manifested in the story and their applicability to society today.

The love of the soil; something that runs through most of Steinbeck's works.

The cruelty of the treatment of the tenant farmers by the landowners and the subsequent cruelty migrant workers faced during the migration to California and while trying to work in the state.

Strength in unity—of the family, the community, with one's fellow workers.

The importance of adaptability to change in survival.

The virtue of anger as an antidote to the dehumanizing of the poor and indigent.

- **RSL.9-10.1** Cite strong and thorough textual evidence to support analysis of what the text says explicitly as well as inferences drawn from the text.
- **RSL.9-10.2** Determine a theme or central idea of a text and analyze in detail its development over the course of the text, including how it emerges and is shaped and refined by specific details; provide an objective summary of the text.
- **RSL.9-10.3** Analyze how complex characters develop over the course of a text, interact with other characters, and advance the plot or develop the theme.
- **RSL.9-10.4** Determine the meaning of words and phrases as they are used in the text, including figurative and connotative meanings; analyze the cumulative impact of specific word choices on meaning and tone.
- **RSL.9-10.7** Analyze the representation of a subject or a key scene in two different artistic mediums, including what is emphasized or absent in each treatment.
- **RSL.9-10.10** By the end of grade 9 read and comprehend literature, including stories, dramas, and poems, in the grades 9–10 text complexity band proficiently, with scaffolding as needed at the high end of the range. By the end of grade 10, read and comprehend literature, including stories, dramas, and poems, at the high end of the grades 9–10 text complexity band independently and proficiently.
- **RSL.11-12.1** Cite strong and thorough textual evidence to support analysis of what the text says explicitly as well as inferences drawn from the text, including determining where the text leaves matters uncertain.
- **RSL.11-12.2** Determine two or more themes or central ideas of a text and analyze their development over the course of the text, including how they interact and build on one another to produce a complex account; provide an objective summary of the text.
- **RSL.11-12.3** Analyze the impact of the author's choices regarding how to develop and relate elements of a story or drama.
- **RSL.11-12.4** Determine the meaning of words and phrases as they are used in the text, including figurative and connotative meanings; analyze the impact of specific word choices on meaning and tone, including words with multiple meanings or language that is particularly fresh, engaging, or beautiful.
- **RSL.11-12.7** Analyze multiple interpretations of a story, drama, or poem, evaluating how each version interprets the source text.

  RSL.11-12.10 By the end of grade 11, read and comprehend literature, including stories, dramas, and poems, in the grades 11–CCR text complexity band proficiently, with scaffolding as needed at the high end of the range. By the end of grade 12, read and comprehend literature, including stories, dramas, and poems, at the high end of the grades 11–CCR text complexity band independently and proficiently.
- **WS.9-10.1** Write arguments to support claims in an analysis of substantive topics or texts, using valid reasoning and relevant and sufficient evidence.
- **WS.9-10.2** Write informative/explanatory texts to examine and convey complex ideas, concepts, and information clearly and accurately through the effective selection, organization, and analysis of content.
- **WS.9-10.3** Write narratives to develop real or imagined experiences or events using effective technique, well-chosen details, and well-structured event sequences..
- **WS.9-10.4** Produce clear and coherent writing in which the development, organization, and style are appropriate to task, purpose, and audience.
- **WS.9-10.7** Conduct short as well as more sustained research projects to answer a question or solve a problem; narrow or broaden the inquiry when appropriate; synthesize multiple sources on the subject, demonstrating understanding of the subject under investigation.
- **WS.9-10.8** Gather relevant information from multiple authoritative print and digital sources, using advanced searches effectively; assess the usefulness of each source in answering the research question; integrate information into the text selectively to maintain the flow of ideas, avoiding plagiarism and following a standard format for citation.
- **WS.9-10.9** Draw evidence from literary or informational texts to support analysis, reflection, and research.
- **WS.11-12.1** Write arguments to support claims in an analysis of substantive topics or texts, using valid reasoning and relevant and sufficient evidence.
- **WS.11-12.2** Write informative/explanatory texts to examine and convey complex ideas, concepts, and information clearly and accurately through the effective selection, organization, and analysis of content.
- **WS.11-12.3** Write narratives to develop real or imagined experiences or events using effective technique, well-chosen details, and well-structured event sequences.
- **WS.11-12.4** Produce clear and coherent writing in which the development, organization, and style are appropriate to task, purpose, and audience.
- **WS.11-12.7** Conduct short as well as more sustained research projects to answer a question or solve a problem; narrow or broaden the inquiry when appropriate; synthesize multiple sources on the subject, demonstrating understanding of the subject under investigation.
- **WS.11-12.8** Gather relevant information from multiple authoritative print and digital sources, using advanced searches effectively; assess the strengths and limitations of each source in terms of the task, purpose, and audience; integrate information into the text selectively to maintain the flow of ideas, avoiding plagiarism and overreliance on any one source and following a standard format for citation.
- **WS.11-12.9** Draw evidence from literary or informational texts to support analysis, reflection, and research.